Cannabis Oil:

The Ultimate Guide to Using Cannabis Oil for Disease Prevention, Skin Conditions And many More Powerful Health Benefits

Table Of Contents

Introduction

Chapter 1: What You Need To Know About Cannabis Oil

Chapter 2: Proper Usage of Cannabis Oil

Chapter 3: Cannabis Oil For Different Skin Conditions

Chapter 4: Cannabis Oil for Treating Cancers

Chapter 5: Cannabis Oil for Other Common Health Problems

Conclusion

Introduction

I want to thank you and congratulate you for downloading the book, *Cannabis Oil: The Ultimate Guide to Using Cannabis Oil for Disease Prevention, Skin Conditions And many More Powerful Health Benefits.*

This book contains proven steps and strategies on how you'll be able to properly use the medicinal benefits that cannabis oil can provide you with. Here, you'll be provided not just with up to date facts about the latest findings but you'll also learn how to make the oil yourself. After all, some people prefer doing things by themselves to ensure purity and the safety of the product itself when it comes to using it.

Here's an inescapable fact: Despite its bad rep as a recreational drug, certain varieties of the cannabis plant as well as its byproducts can actually significantly improve our health. From helping us with common ailments such as headaches and muscle pain to treating more serious diseases such as cancers and cardiovascular issues, cannabis oil certainly has countless uses and benefits that you can harness with the right guide and information.

Here's a quick overview of what you'll learn from this book:

   ⅄ What cannabis oil is made of
   ⅄ How safe is it for topical and oral use
   ⅄ Different medicinal uses for it

⅄ The proper application and dosage
⅄ Making your own cannabis oil
⅄ Cannabis oil and its effects of skin disorders
⅄ How it can help treat different cancer types
⅄ Using cannabis oil for common health problems
⅄ And so much more!

When it comes to treating our different illnesses, whether it is something that requires a one-time treatment or a continuous one, there are always two options. You can go for something provided over the counter which works well for quite a lot of people. However, there are side effects associated with it that you may not want for yourself. In cases such as those, the other option is to go natural—something that's gentler on our bodies and possesses very little to no side effects at all. Cannabis oil would be able to provide you with that. With regular and appropriate use, you should be able to see improvements in no time.

So go on and learn more about this amazing product today!

Chapter 1: What You Need To Know About Cannabis Oil

Cannabis oil, also known as hemp oil, is a byproduct of the Cannabis plant. It is important to note that while all of the plants that fall under the Cannabis genus can produce oil, it is only the industrial cannabis plant that can be used in producing this particular oil. This is because this plant is specifically cultivated for that purpose and also contains only the minimum amount of psychoactive substances that are typically associated with this plant genus. In fact, it is also free of THC and has very little to no psychoactive properties at all.

The seeds tend to produce some of the best cannabis seed oil but the entire plant itself can be processed for it. Cold pressed oil that hasn't undergone any refinement comes with a rich and nutty flavor, often tinted green naturally. Once it has been refined, however, the oil loses this green color and the flavor becomes more subtle.

As for everyday uses for the product, there are a number of them. Among the most common would be in soaps. It can also be used in lubricants as well as paints. Body care products, especially organic ones, use it as one of the best and most potent moisturizers that nature can provide. It can also be applied directly onto the skin as a treatment for cracks or flaking. Body oils, body creams and even certain perfumes contain a specific amount of this product. For health uses, people have taken to using it as a dietary supplement. It does contain a high amount of essential fatty acids-- comparable to fish and olive oil, as a matter of fact. Much like the other two oils mentioned, cannabis or hemp seed oil is also often used as a garnish in various dishes.

Unrefined cannabis oil actually has a short shelf life and it can quickly go rancid unless you store it in dark, tinted containers. Refrigerating it also helps in slowing down this process. Typically, people purchase this product in small amounts so nothing goes to waste. One important thing you have to remember is that cannabis oil is not suitable for cooking. It has a very low smoking point and cooking it in high heat can also change its chemical composition. Refined cannabis seed oil lasts longer but most of the benefits associated with it are no longer present after it has been processed.

So is it legal?

Cannabis remains to be a controversial crop in many regions of the world because of different concerns regarding its effects on people. In fact, there are places wherein the mere cultivation of the plant is completely banned but the products produced from it such as oil, paper, and garments are legally traded. In some places, only industrial hemp is permitted.

There are also nations wherein the cultivation of all the plants under the genus is freely permitted, thinking that this technique is far more efficient than outright banning it. It should also be noted that wild hemp is not uncommon in some regions of the world thus making the enforcement of bans even harder. To be sure, however, do your research about the area you reside in. In some cases, cannabis regulations can vary from one state to another.

Different Uses for Cannabis Oil:

Here's a quick fact: You can easily substitute petroleum jelly with cannabis oil when it comes to your skin and hair. As a matter of fact, the latter is far more beneficial and herbal. Let's take a quick look at the different medicinal uses for it:

- Because it is all natural, it can be used as a moisturizer and applied directly onto the skin after a bath or a shower. It can also be used as a massage oil, effectively nourishing the skin and keeping it hydrated throughout the day-- especially if you spend a lot of time under the sun or during the colder times of the year.

- For insomnia problems. It helps patients fall asleep smoother and quicker. While improving the quality as well as duration of their sleep. Cannabis oil can also help with promoting deep sleep. For anxiety issues, often related to insomnia, it helps in relaxing both the mind and body. It can also help in relieving headaches as well as migraines without having to resort to over the counter pain relievers.

- This oil can also help in digestion problems such as the lack of appetite. Other things it can provide a solution to include irritable bowel syndrome, stomach ache colic, balancing the intestinal flora, vomiting, nausea, constipation, diarrhea, and Crohn's disease. Recent studies have shown that it can also help in preventing colon as well as intestinal cancer.

- Improves circulation as well as blood pressure. It is known to protect from cardiovascular disease along with regulating blood pressure issues. The oil can also protect the heart and at the same time, help in properly balancing different cardiac functions. If you're suffering from high blood pressure, taking this oil can help in lowering that along with your cholesterol and blood lipid levels. Lastly, it is known to be able to help in regulating glycemia and reducing high levels of blood sugar.

- Pain and auto-immune diseases. Recent studies on the effects of cannabis oil when it comes to cancer have shown that it can significantly reduce pain (especially during chemotherapy) as well as help address the patient's lack of appetite. It can also be used as a treatment for multiple sclerosis. For people who have asthma and epilepsy, cannabis oil can also be used as a form of treatment. And because of the fact that it can actually help in boosting the immune system, it also lowers the chances of certain illnesses from repeating. It all depends on regular use.

Those are just some of the most common medicinal uses for cannabis oil, but how do we actually use it? This is one of the most important aspects of utilizing cannabis oil as proper usage also ensures maximum benefits.

Chapter 2: Proper Usage of Cannabis Oil

Topical Use:

Cannabis, as we've pointed out earlier, has long been in use when it comes to different medical issues. Typically, there are two different ways of taking it: Topical and Oral. Topical medicines are, of course, applied onto the targeted area and then absorbed through the skin. It is the less invasive of the two options and is often used to reduce the amount of possible side effects. Recent studies have shown that for certain purposes, such as using cannabis oil for skin conditions, a topical application is more effective at reducing symptoms. Many patients who have tried this method before also found that the effects can be felt much quicker when compared to taking the oil orally.

The skin is the largest organ we have and is fully capable of absorbing medicine that is applied to it. Most people would suggest topical application because this also means that the preparation won't affect the brain receptors thus eliminating any effects that it might have on it. That said, it is also important to note that very rarely do people experienced that effect of being "high" when using cannabis oil. It all depends on the preparation as well as the dosage.

Oral Use:

For situations wherein cannabis oil is needed to be taken orally, dosage becomes even more important. The first thing you need to consider is the purpose; what are you taking the oil for? It would be helpful to ask your physician about this and allow him to prescribe the right dosage for you and your needs. Typically, however, it would take at least 60 grams of cannabis oil to deal with most cancer types. The average person would take about 90 days to consume this, ingesting 3 doses of the oil each day.

Preparation is also important and there are many different ways through which this is done. We'll provide you with an easy to follow guide later on.

As for the side effects of orally ingesting cannabis oil, the most that people have experienced would be the feeling of sleepiness and calmness. Of course, this only helps in furthering your body's recovery from the illness. Lethargy during the first week of using it is also a common occurrence but this effect would eventually diminish as you continue on.

Making The Oil:

With the help of an easy to follow guide, you should be able to make your own cannabis oil-- this is if you're not keen on purchasing premade ones and would rather that you do it yourself.

Tools Needed:

- Odor respirator mask
- Non-latex safety gloves
- High heat gloves or oven mitts
- Safety glasses
- Large funnel
- Large stainless steel bowls
- Large bottles for holding mixtures
- Stainless measuring cups
- Pyrex storage dish
- Stainless mesh strainer

- Stainless mixing spoons

- High temperature silicone scrape

- Coffee filters

- 99% (or higher) Isopropyl alcohol

- Thermometer

- Electric rice cooker

- Table fan

- Electric warmer

- Empty pill capsules

- Oral dispensing syringes

Procedure:

1. Purchase and dry your plants. Make sure that you get the best ones you can afford. Remember that the better its quality, the better your oil will be as well. Another thing you have to remember is to dry the plants well. You can use UV lighting to achieve this or simply dry them naturally.

2. Once the plants are dried, place this on the bowl then dampen it with the solvent you've chosen. The solvent will further remove the THC from your plants. Typically, it would take about two gallons of it to completely strip the THC off.

3. Crush the plant gently. If it has been dried properly, doing this should be quite easy even if it has already been dampened by your solvent. As you do this, the THC gets stripped from the plant and is then absorbed by the solvent. Do this for at least 5 to 10 minutes.

4. Once you're done with that, filter all of the cannabis and separate it from the solvent oil mix. Set the oil aside. Using the same plants, pour more solvent onto it and repeat step #3. This should help you completely remove the THC off of it.

5. Repeat the filtering process and add your freshly crushed solvent-oil mix into first batch. Use a strainer for this to make sure that none of the plant material gets into the liquid. At this point, prepare your bottle that will hold the oil as well.

6. Take your funnel and line it with a coffee filter before putting it on the bottle's nozzle. Make sure everything is clean and sanitized before you begin pouring the solvent-oil mix into it. The filter is meant to strain out any remaining traces of the plant. It would be best to repeat this process at least 2 to 3 times to make sure that you get pure oil and none of the plant bits in it.

7. In this step, we will be boiling away the solvent from your oil. Take your rice cooker. Add your solvent-oil mix into it but make sure that you don't fill it more than ¾ full. Set it on high heat and watch as the solvent-oil mix inside the cooker slowly lessens. Once this begins to happen, continue adding more of the mix until you've managed to put it all in there. When there's only about an inch left, take your mitts and pick up the container. Gently swirl its contents around.

Note: Make sure the area you're in is well ventilated, or if you can, head outside so that the fumes don't get trapped. Otherwise, a puddle of the solvent might begin to pool around or under the rice cooker. Also, do stay away from anything that's flammable and make sure to wear your mask so you don't end up inhaling the fumes.

8. Before you remove the oil from the rice cooker, make sure that all of your solvent has completely boiled away. Once you've checked, gently pour the collected oil into a glass container. Do this slowly and carefully.

9. Next, you have to place your container over a heating device to allow the Co2 to evaporate from the oil. This might take a few hours. Once there are no more bubbles or any kind of activity on the surface of your oil, it is ready for use. A quick note, the more you heat the oil over very gentle heat, the more sedative it will become.

10.   Once the oil cools off it, would be dark brown in color and has the consistency of molasses which is quite thick. When spread on paper, it should be a nice golden color. Be sure to store your oil at room temperature and away from humidity and light in order to maintain its freshness. You should be able to easily tell when the oil has turned rancid and is no longer usable.

Chapter 3: Cannabis Oil For Different Skin Conditions

Among the known benefits that cannabis oil has is its ability to treat different skin conditions. This can be attributed to a number of different things. To begin with, the oil itself is actually rich in essential fatty acids. If you've been doing your research, that alone is a signifier that this particular cannabis plant byproduct is actually quite healthy for the body. According to certain studies, cannabis oil can actually help in keeping moisture locked in our skin as well as prevent premature aging. Besides these, it can also be very beneficial when used to treat certain skin conditions such as acne, eczema and psoriasis.

Cannabis oil is comprised of omega-3 and omega-6 essential fatty acids, the combination of which is known to be necessary for overall skin health as well as healthy cell production. The modern man's average diet lack a proper balance of these thus resulting in a number of different skin conditions which, left untreated, can be detrimental to the person's health.

Cannabis oil is also known to be a rich source of gamma-linoleic acid or GLA. This is another variety of the omega-6 fatty acid and also contains a number of properties that are beneficial to the skin. For example, it s anti-inflammatory and is also very moisturizing. GLA is ore popularly known as borage or primrose oil. As for adding it to your daily diet, the opinion is still divided.

Cannabis oil as a cure for acne: When it comes to the effects of the oil on acne, the opinions are highly divided. One thing is for certain, however. The oil itself contains high levels of anti-inflammatory properties which can significantly reduce both the redness and swelling of your acne. It is also a powerful antioxidant which can significantly help in clearing up your skin as well as delaying the signs of aging upon it. Think of it as a serum and a little goes a long way when it comes to using the oil for this purpose. It can also be used as both cleanser and moisturizer. The best part is it will not clog your pores so you don't have to worry about your acne getting worse or the development of other skin issues such as whiteheads and blackheads.

Cannabis oil as a cure for eczema: There have been numerous studies wherein doctors saw the significant effects that cannabis oil has on people with eczema issues. The first of these effects would be the reduction in both itching and dryness, two of the biggest issues that people have with this skin condition. It can also help improve the symptoms in patients much better and faster when compared to olive oil. Another important thing to note, when it comes to using over the counter products for eczema, is that it the issue tends to flare up due to the different additives and ingredients in the product itself. Chemical food additives, preservatives, as well as scents can further worsen the symptoms so it is best to use something that's completely natural when treating the problem. There are 2 ways of taking cannabis oil for this purpose. The first is to orally consume 2 tablespoons of it each day for at least 2 months. The second is to topically apply it to the problem areas.

Cannabis oil for psoriasis: For this particular skin condition, cannabis oil can also significant help in easing the symptoms associated with it along with healing the broken skin. It can help reduce the itchiness, redness through the use of its anti-inflammatory and antioxidant properties. With regular use, it can also alleviate and minimize its appearance on the skin. The best bit? It can also serve as a moisturizer to reduce the flaking and if mixed with your sunscreen, it could help keep the skin from drying out during the day.

Chapter 4: Cannabis Oil for Treating Cancers

What is the science behind cannabis oil and cancer? It has been proven that it has great effects when it comes to treating a large number of ailments and in recent studies, it has also been proven to be beneficial when it comes to treating cancer. Cannabinoids, a property contained in the oil, is being considered as one of the most potent natural disease and cancer fighting treatments currently available. This property also help in activating cannabinoid receptors which are naturally in our body. Together with endocannabinoids, which is naturally produced by our bodies, they help in creating a healthy environment and also play a role in many different bodily processes.

Cannabinoids also play a role when it comes to improving immune system function and regeneration. In fact, the body regenerates better and faster when it is saturated with phyto-cannabinoids. Not only that, it can also help in reducing the amount of cancer cells in the body whilst aiding in the recovery of a compromised immune system. For this purpose, studies have shown that consuming the oil orally is the most effective way of delivering the good stuff to where you need it.

To be able to understand how this works better, below is a quick overview of the different effects that cannabis oil has on different cancer types when used regularly and properly:

Brain Cancer – In a study conducted by one University in Madrid, it was shown that cannabinoids, along with THC, was capable of inhibiting tumor growth. The delivery also proved to be very safe with zero psychoactive effects on the patient. Other studies looked into its effects on the different biochemical events in acute neuronal damage as well as in slowly progressing neurodegenerative diseases. This resulted in the finding that, yet again, cannabinoids are capable of protecting the brain from neurodegeneration. Both discoveries are important when it comes to learning more about its effects on brain cancer in that it can significantly drop the viability of glioma cells (brain tumors) as a whole.

Breast Cancer – Quite a number of studies have been done on the effects of cannabis oil on breast cancer and a lot of which of have all proven to be positive. Among the positive discoveries that they have made would be the fact that cannabinoids are capable of inhibiting the proliferation as well as invasion of breast cancer cells. Besides this, it is also shown to be capable of significantly reducing the tumor mass. Another thing that they have learned about the component is that it can also induce cancer cell apoptosis as well as impair tumor angiogenesis (both of which are very good things). These discoveries back up the theory that cannabinoid based therapies are a great option for managing breast cancer.

Lung Cancer – When it comes to lung cancer, researchers have learned that the properties contained in cannabis oil were able to inhibit the epithelial growth which induces the migration of lung cancer cells. It was also able to decrease cancer cell invasiveness, something that's quite crucial when it comes to managing the disease and helping the patient towards recovery. At the moment, further studies are being done on its effects when it comes to controlling both the metastasis and growth of certain lung cancers. Nevertheless, it is still a recommended form of treatment for the problem.

Prostate Cancer – Acting through cannabinoid receptors in our body, cannabis oil was able to show a reduction in cancer cells affecting the prostate as well as inhibit cell viability. It was also able to induce prostate carcinoma cell aptosis.

Blood Cancer – When it comes to blood cancer, studies prove that cannabinoids are capable of inhibiting growth and at the same time, inducing aptosis in matle cell lymphoma. The same can be said when it comes to leukemia cells and many of these doctors and researchers recommend it as a regular natural treatment for the disease.

Oral Cancer – There's not much research into this yet but what little study has been done was able to prove that cannabis oil can become a potent inhibitor of cellular respiration and is also very toxic towards highly malignant oral tumors. Basically, it can help in slowly breaking it down.

Liver Cancer – For liver cancer, they have proven that cannabinoids help in reducing the viability of the human HCC cell lines (aka the human hepatocellular liver carcinoma cell line) thus reducing its growth at the same time.

Pancreatic Cancer – When it comes to this, researchers have determined that our cannabinoid receptors tend to be expressed in both human pancreatic tumor cell lines and tumor biopsies at higher levels than the normal pancreatic tissue. Their test results have shown that cannabis oil administration was able to induce apoptosis and was also central in reducing the growth of tumor cells along with inhibiting it from spreading further.

Do note that these are just some of the cancer types that cannabis oil can be used for. There are a lot more in this list but at the moment, many of them are still undergoing research and further study so that more concrete evidence can be provided when it comes to the viability of the oil as treatment for it.

Chapter 5: Cannabis Oil for Other Common Health Problems

I. For Diabetes:

- Cannabis oil can help in stabilizing your blood sugar.

- It also has anti-inflammatory properties which can help in easing some of the arterial inflammation that is commonly experienced by those who have diabetes.

- Its neuroprotective effects also help in thwarting any nerve inflammation as well as reduce the pain brought on by neuropathy by activating different receptors in the brain and body.

- The oil also contains anti-spasmodic agents which help in relieving both muscle cramps as well as the pain associated with gastrointestinal disorders.

- It can also act as a vasodilator which would help keep the blood vessels open as well as improve the circulation. Over time, it would also contribute to a lower blood pressure which is vital for all diabetics.

- Besides being ingested orally, it can also be used as a topical cream which would help in relieving neuropathic pain as well as any tingling in both hands and feet of the patient.

II. Migraines and Headaches

- When it comes to migraines, there are several possible causes for it. This includes: stress, fatigue, hunger, hormonal changes, medication as well as eating highly processed foods on the regular (including canned foods as well as those that contain high amounts of chemical additives). Typical treatments for this problem could range from taking an analgesic or in some cases, prescribed medication. Prophylactic measures would include getting enough sleep and rest, reducing the amount of stressors in the environment as well as switching to a diet that contains the proper nutrition.

How can cannabis oil help? What you need to do is add it to your everyday diet as a part of the preventive measures you're taking against migraines. Its omega 3 fatty acid content have anti-inflammatory properties which are great when it comes to improving your overall emotional health, your brain function as well as your cardiovascular health. In some cases, the oil can also help improve the quality of your sleep thus allowing you to get more of the rest that you need. The only issue here is that this essential fatty acid is often lacking in the average person's diet so you have to introduce a supplement to balance it out. The great bit is that there are numerous ways through which you can add cannabis oil to your every day meals without needing to change a lot of it.

Remember...

To note the right amount and dosage of the cannabis oil that you need before using it for these purposes. You would want to consult with an expert or a physician who is familiar with its use to make sure that you're getting everything right. Only then will you be able to benefit from its healing properties.

Another thing you can do is add a bit more research to what you already know through this book. Look for other complementary supplements that you can partner with the cannabis oil which would further enhance its benefits. There are many things that you can do, just take the initiative in finding them.

Lastly, going all natural when it comes to treatments that you have to take every day is still the best route to go. In the long run, you wouldn't have to worry about side effects or damaging your body even more. After all, you have to help it recover while you obliterate what might be ailing you.

Good luck!

Conclusion

Thank you again for downloading this book!

I hope this book was able to help you to better understand what cannabis oil is, its benefits as well as how safe it is— quite unlike what you might have heard or been told beforehand.

The next step is to put what you have learned into action and start using it as an all natural alternative to the typical cures and treatments that you use on yourself. Not only is it safer to use, it also tends to be more affordable whether you make it yourself or buy it premade. Choosing the right one is also something you should consider and for this, talk to experts or even a physician who's familiar with its use. They should be able to provide you with extra information when it comes to properly choosing one for your condition and needs. Remember that each person is different and as such, there are certain things that you must consider.

Keep it mind that it all depends on how you make use of it and if you follow the guides you've been provided with. Too much of a good thing can also become detrimental to your improvement in the long run. Also, this is not an overnight cure. It is a part of the process and you must give it some time before you see any results. Discipline, regular use and the right kind of attitude should help you in reaping the different health benefits that cannabis oil can provide.

Finally, if you enjoyed this book, please take the time to share your thoughts and post a review on Amazon. It'd be greatly appreciated!

Thank you and good luck!

Printed in Great Britain
by Amazon.co.uk, Ltd.,
Marston Gate.